POCKET GUIDE TO
Pretty Stitches

T0356884

Pocket Guide to Pretty Stitches

Landauer Publishing, www.landauerpub.com,
is an imprint of Fox Chapel Publishing Company, Inc.

Project Team
Acquisitions Editor: Amelia Johanson
Managing Editor: Gretchen Bacon
Editor: Sherry Vitolo
Designer: Wendy Reynolds

ISBN 978-1-63981-112-0

Library of Congress Control Number: 2024945382

To learn more about the other great books from Fox Chapel Publishing, or to find
a retailer near you, call toll-free 800-457-9112, send mail to 903 Square Street,
Mount Joy, PA 17552, or visit us at www.FoxChapelPublishing.com.

We are always looking for talented authors. To submit an idea, please send a brief
inquiry to acquisitions@foxchapelpublishing.com.

The following images are from Shutterstock.com: 6, 7 top: Daria Yachmeneva;
7 bottom: Amam ka; 9: Lara Joy; 10: Suvi Sivula; 11: Jen Bray Photography; 12:
MRizly; 15: Yasji; 17: Sinn P. Photography; 18: Anna Kepa; 19: Unwanus; 20:
Tatiana Buzmakova; 21 left: Lipskiy; 21 right: KrimKate; 23: Africa Studio

Printed in China

First printing

POCKET GUIDE TO
Pretty Stitches

Carry-Along Guide to
Visible Mending & Embroidery Stitches

Karen
Hemingway

Landauer Publishing

Contents

Introduction

Embroidery includes a vast array of stitches and techniques, and the craft has long been used in conjunction with visible mending practices and clothing repair to breathe new life into flawed pieces. Clever creators use embroidery to cover holes, stains, and patches with beautiful flowers or patterns, personalize clothing that might otherwise have gone into the donation pile, or fix pieces with gorgeous stitching in contrasting colors (think of stunning Japanese Sashiko stitching or Indian kantha stitching).

Visible mending embraces imperfections and promotes sustainability, while letting you add a bit more personality to your garments! This book walks you through what you need to know to begin embroidering and artfully mending your clothing. First, you'll take a look at the different types of fabrics you may need to work with and how to prepare those fabrics. Then, you'll learn different methods for transferring embroidery designs (whether intricate drawings or detailed geometric patterns), and what to look for in needles and threads. Finally, there's a quick guide to 50 stitches that work equally well in standalone embroidered art and visible mending.

A contrasting patch and some simple hand stitching can turn an old shirt into something brand new.

As you explore the art of visible mending and embroidery, remember that there are no strict rules. Allow yourself the freedom to experiment and use any imperfections as a starting point for creativity. Embrace sustainability and self-expression, with the tips and stitches in this book as your guide.

Japanese boro stitching is a true celebration of the artistry of repairing and patching clothing.

Your patch can be as simple as a stylish jumble of stitches in a striking red-and-white thread.

Preparing Your Fabric

Creating a brand-new piece of wall art with a fresh fabric background may require slightly different preparation from decoratively patching a hole in your favorite pair of jeans, but most of the tricks are the same.

- When cutting out background fabric for an art piece, add a margin of at least 3" (7.6cm) all around the outside of the design area to allow for mounting. When patching a clothing item, be sure to leave extra fabric around the outside of the patch (at least ½" [1.3cm]) until you've finished securing it and stitching the design. Once you're finished stitching, trim away any excess fabric to reduce bulk.

- Silks, satin, and lawns will need to be reinforced with a second layer of fabric to support the weight of the stitches. Cut a piece of muslin 3" (7.6cm) larger all around. Center the muslin on the backing and baste it into place, working diagonally from corner to corner, across the center lines and around the edge. Where the embroidery is a small part of a larger piece, trim away the surplus muslin so that it only backs the embroidery.

Many types of cloth fray
along the edges, so it's best
to secure those edges with
stitching or masking tape.

When patching clothing items, try to choose patch fabric with similar fiber content, thickness, and texture. (Color matching is optional!)

- When choosing fabric or material to patch a clothing item, try to choose fabric that is similar in thickness, stretchiness, and texture to the clothing item. Thinner patches may distort the patched area, while thicker patches may add too much bulk or weight.

- Choose patching fabric that exactly matches your fabric's color, or choose patches that creatively contrast against the original color.

- If necessary, wash and press linen or cotton to prevent any later color run or shrinkage.

- Some cloth, and most canvas, will fray along cut edges, so hem edges or zigzag stitch loosely woven fabric edges and bind canvas with masking tape. If you are fixing a piece of clothing, you may want to trim any frayed threads or edges.

- Always mark the center of the fabric. Lightly press it in half lengthwise and widthwise to create creases. If possible, work a line of contrasting running stitches along each crease, following the weave carefully. This will help you accurately position the design and establish a good tension when mounting the fabric. If you don't want to use temporary stitches to mark clothing you're mending or embroidering, simple creases or lines marked with removable marking tools are a good option for aligning your designs.

Mounting Fabric

Lightweight wooden embroidery hoops are portable and the best option for small-scale work, including anything involved with clothing embellishment or visible mending.

Simple wooden embroidery hoops are the best for working on clothing items. They don't have ridges like most plastic hoops, so they're less likely to damage your fabric.

Properly mounted fabric will have a taut surface that's easy for you to stitch through.

To mount your cloth, loosen the screw and separate the two rings. Especially if you're working on a piece of clothing, wrap the inner ring with bias or seam binding to protect the fabric and prevent it from slipping. Place the fabric over the inner ring, and slide the outer ring into place. Stretch the fabric gently until it is taut like a drumhead, check that any guidelines are straight, then tighten the screw to secure it.

Working On Evenweave Fabrics

Evenweave fabrics—linen, canvas, and Aida cloth—are used for needlepoint, cross-stitch, and other techniques where the stitches need to be evenly spaced and of regular length. They are woven with the same number of threads in each direction to create an even grid across the surface. The thicker these threads, the greater the "count" or number of threads per inch. This can vary from fine 24-count linen down to chunky 7-count canvas: high-count fabrics require small stitches made with delicate threads, while low-count fabrics require bolder stitches made with thick threads.

Use a blunt needle and count the threads carefully to produce regular stitches:

- For **horizontal stitches**, count across the vertical threads.

- For **upright stitches**, count across the horizontal threads.

- For **diagonal stitches**, count the intersections where the two sets of thread cross.

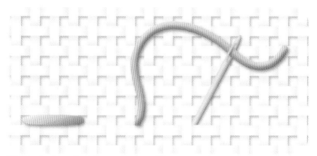

Working horizontal stitches on evenweave fabric.

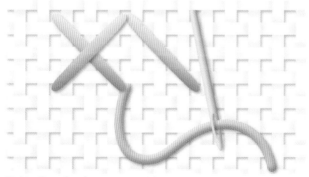

Working diagonal stitches on evenweave fabric.

Transferring the Design

Whether you follow a project or create your own pattern, you'll have to transfer the design onto the background fabric. This can be done in various ways, including freehand drawing, tracing the design directly onto the fabric, using carbon paper, or working with water-soluble transfer paper or stabilizer. The most appropriate method will depend on the type of stitches, threads, and fabric being used.

Keep the following items in mind when deciding on a transfer method:

- The outline must be accurate, and none of the marked lines should be visible on the completed embroidery.

- You can use a photocopier to enlarge or reduce designs if needed.

- To center your design, draw a horizontal and a vertical line to divide it into quarters. Match these guidelines to horizontal and vertical guidelines on the surface to be stitched. If you're working on a new project, you should already have added guidelines to the background fabric with contrasting running stitches.

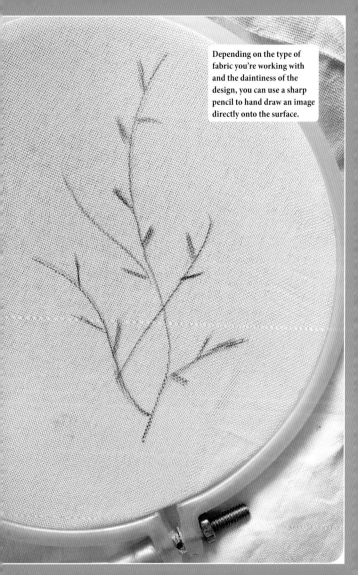

Depending on the type of fabric you're working with and the daintiness of the design, you can use a sharp pencil to hand draw an image directly onto the surface.

Hand Tracing

Drawing directly onto the fabric is quick and straightforward. You can place sheer fabrics directly over a design to trace it. For denser cloth, you'll need to shine light through the design and the fabric. Tape the design to a window, blank computer screen, or lightbox, then tape the fabric over the design and trace it.

On cotton or linen, you can trace the design with a sharp pencil if the planned stitches are not too delicate.

Water-soluble felt-tip pens create lines that disappear completely. Always follow the manufacturer's directions and test a sample piece first: not all fabrics are suitable for use with these pens.

You can easily improvise a lightbox by resting a sheet of glass on two stacks of books and setting up a lamp or flashlight in the space below.

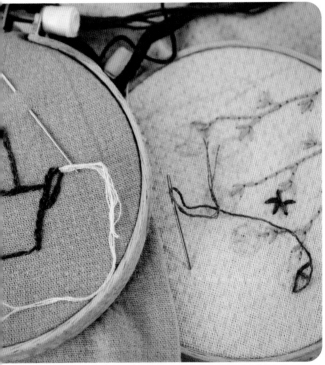

Pens specifically made for use with fabric are a great option for hand sketching or tracing your design.

Air-erasable fabric pens are useful for non-colorfast materials, but you may have to redraw the lines (or sew very quickly).

A chalk pencil is ideal for simple outlines.

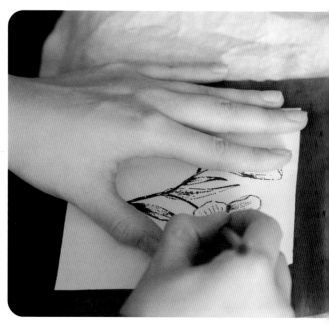

Carbon/Transfer Paper

You can use carbon or transfer paper to trace designs onto your fabric if you don't have a lightbox. Use light paper for dark fabrics and dark paper for light fabrics.

Tape the fabric onto a flat surface, tape the carbon or transfer paper face down on top of the fabric, then tape the design on top of the paper. Trace over the design with a ballpoint pen to transfer the image.

Once you've finished stitching your design, just brush away any remaining carbon marks.

Water-Soluble Stabilizer

Printable, water-soluble stabilizer is another alternative. Designs can be drawn or printed directly onto the "paper." This stabilizer has a tacky back that lightly adheres to your fabric, and you stitch directly through it. These stabilizers are especially useful if you are working to patch or mend clothing. They can help create a more secure base for your stitches until you've finished your work. Once the embroidery is done, you can submerge your piece in water to dissolve the stabilizer.

◄ Apply steady pressure when tracing a pattern using carbon or transfer paper. It's not recommended to avoid taping down your pieces, as they could shift while you trace and add marks to the fabric where you don't want them.

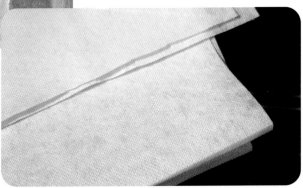

Water-soluble stabilizers are similar in texture to the interfacing used for quilting and other sewing techniques. It both transfers the image and creates a solid foundation for your stitches.

Needle Guide

Embroidery or crewel needles have long eyes to accommodate most threads. They come in different sizes, and the length you use is a matter of personal preference.

A **fine tapestry or "ball point" needle** has a blunt end. These are best to use with evenweave fabrics and are helpful for making interlaced stitches.

A **round-eyed quilting or "between" needle**, which does not widen at the top, can slip more easily through coiled threads to create knotted stitches.

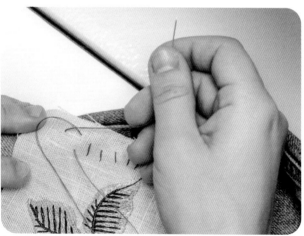

Depending on the materials you're working with and the fix you are making, you may prefer using a standard hand-sewing needle.

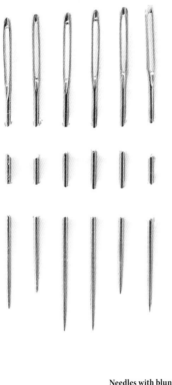

◄ The longer eye of an embroidery needle can fit many different thread thicknesses. Work with the needle length that is best for you.

Needles with blunter tips are useful for interweaving threads in interlaced stitches.

Thread Guide

There is an inspiring selection of threads to use for free embroidery or mending.

Stranded embroidery floss, which is mercerized to give it a sheen, is the most versatile: you can separate the six strands and use them singly or in combination to create different stitch thicknesses. By working with several strands of different colors, you can create subtle blended effects. **Rayon floss** is a brilliant synthetic thread that is also stranded.

The single twisted thread of shiny **pearl cotton** adds texture to stitches, while **coton à broder** is smoother and has a subtle gleam. These two threads are available in skeins or balls of various weights.

Flower thread is a fine matte thread, while **soft embroidery thread** is thicker and, unsurprisingly, softer.

Silk thread is more expensive but produces glorious effects.

Wool yarns intended for canvas work—**tapestry, Persian, and crewel threads**—can all be used for free embroidery or mending. They're especially useful for stitching on wool backgrounds or fabrics.

Six-stranded embroidery floss is available in almost any color you can imagine and is so versatile!

Stitches to Know

The following stitches are perfect for decorative embroidery work of all sorts, including for livening up your clothing or using visible mending to patch holes, cover stains, or generally fix up older pieces. Remember that your stitches should all be worked at an even tension and consistent length. For example, the links in a row of chain stitch should all be the same size, satin stitches should be the same distance apart, and the slanted stitches of herringbone should all lie at identical angles. Try practicing these stitches on evenweave linen to get the feel of even stitching before working on plain weave fabric or incorporating them into your clothing fixes.

Practice making even stitches on plain fabric, then you'll be perfectly prepared to incorporate them into your art and your mending!

Running Stitch

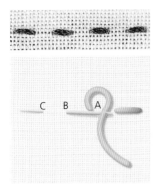

Use this stitch as an outline or a filling in straight or curved lines. Bring the needle up at A, insert it at B, and bring it out again at C to make the next stitch. Continue in this way, making stitches of regular length that are evenly spaced.

Whipped Running Stitch (Cordonnet)

This stitch is particularly suitable for spirals and curved motifs. To whip a running stitch, thread a tapestry needle with contrasting thread. Bring the needle up at A under the first stitch. Then slip the needle down behind the second stitch. Continue whipping the running stitches in this way to the end of the line.

Back Stitch (Point de Sable)

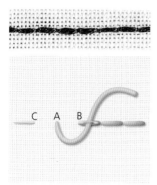

This can be worked in straight or curved lines. Bring the needle up at A and make a short back stitch to the right, inserting the needle at B. Bring the needle up at C, equidistant from A, and insert it again at A to make another back stitch. Continue in this way, keeping all the stitches the same length.

Threaded Back Stitch

The plain back stitch can be embellished by interweaving in one or more contrasting colors. Using a tapestry needle, come up at A under the first back stitch. Slide the needle down under the second stitch and then up under the third. Repeat this weaving process to the end of the back-stitched row, then take the thread to the back to secure.

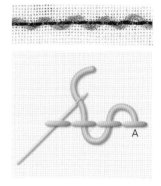

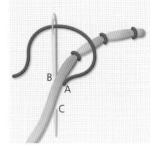

Couching (Simple Laid Work)

Corded, metallic, and other threads that are too thick to stitch through the fabric can be anchored on top of the fabric with small stitches in a finer thread. This produces a bold, flexible line that can also be worked in rows as a filling. Bring both threads up at the start of the row. Using the fine thread, bring the needle up at A, and then take it back down at B to make a stitch at right angles to the couched thread. Bring the needle up again at C ready to make the next stitch. Keep the tension even by holding the couched thread down with the tip of your thumb, and make the couching stitches at equal intervals. Finish both threads off at the back of the fabric.

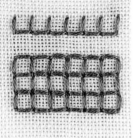 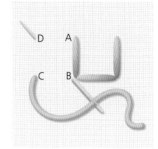

Paris Stitch (Pin Stitch)

This linear stitch, which looks like blanket stitch (page 45), can be used as a border or in rows to produce a square grid filling. Keep the stitches equal in length for a regular look. Make an upright stitch from A down to B. Bring the needle up at C, level with B, and then re-insert it at B. Bring the needle out again above C, at D, level with A. Make the next straight stitch from D to C and repeat these two stitches to the end, finishing with an upright stitch.

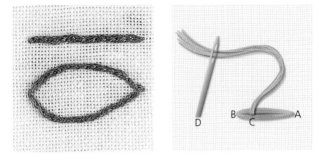

Split Stitch (Kensington Outline Stitch)

This stitch gives a smooth, flexible line that can be used for outlines, as the foundation for raised satin stitch, and, in rows, as a filling. Use a sharp needle and an even number of strands of a loosely woven thread that can easily be divided—stranded floss or crewel wool is ideal. Start with a straight stitch from A to B. Bring the needle up through the first stitch, at C, and insert it again at D to complete the second stitch. Continue in the same way.

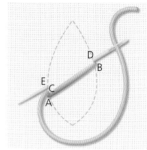

Satin Stitch (Damask Stitch)

This filling gives a smooth, shiny surface. Starting at the widest point of the shape, stitch diagonally from A to B, then C to D, placing the stitches close together. Continue upward from E, varying the length as necessary. Bring the needle out again below A and work down in the same way to cover the remaining space.

Raised Satin Stitch

Work split stitches (page 29) around the outline of the shape to be filled to give extra depth to the satin stitch. For a straight band, work the satin stitches at right angles to the outline. They should be so close together that no fabric is visible.

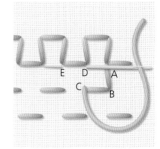

Japanese Darning

One of many beautiful Japanese filling stitches, this is traditionally worked in white thread on indigo fabric (but can be worked in your preferred colors). The foundation rows consist of running stitches (page 25) in which the spaces are slightly shorter than the stitches. Work the second and subsequent rows so that each stitch lies directly below a space. These horizontal rows of stitches are then joined with slightly sloping stitches. On the second row, start with a pair of stitches from A to B and from C to D, then come out again at E for the next pair. Repeat to the end of this and the remaining rows.

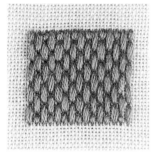 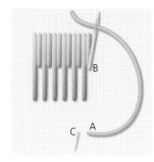

Brick Stitch

This solid or shaded filling is worked in interlocking rows of satin stitches. Starting at the left, work a row of alternating long and short straight stitches to give a straight line along the top edge. Start the second row with a stitch from A to B and bring the needle up again at C for the next stitch. Work all the stitches on this and subsequent rows of the same length and in the spaces between the stitches on the previous row. Continue working downward, and then finish with a final row of both long and short stitches.

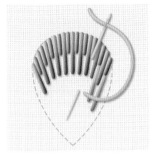

Long and Short Stitch

A more three-dimensional version of brick stitch (page 32), this shaded filling has traditionally been used to give subtle shading on petals and leaves. It looks best when worked in stranded floss, which gives a smooth surface. Work the first row in alternating long and short straight stitches, angling them toward the center of the motif. Fill in the next and subsequent rows with lines of straight stitch all the same length, each row in a progressively darker or lighter shade of thread and tapering off to a point.

Pekinese Stitch (Forbidden Stitch or Chinese Stitch)

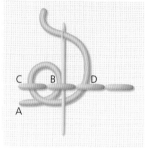

For this more complex interlaced stitch, first work a foundation row of back stitches (page 26). Using a tapestry needle and now working from left to right, come up just below the first stitch at A. Slide the needle up under the second stitch at B and back down under the first stitch at C. Draw the thread through to make a loop. Now make the second loop in the same way, taking the needle up under the third stitch at D and back down under the second stitch at B with the needle on top of the loop being made. Repeat to the end of the back-stitched row.

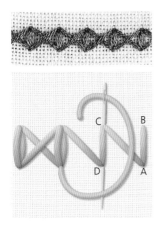

Zigzag Stitch (Triangle Stitch)

Work this stitch in two journeys, from right to left and then back again. Each row is made up of alternating upright and sloping stitches, which together form a pattern of wide cross stitches. Vary the height and spacing of the uprights for a different look. Start with a straight vertical stitch from A up to B, and then make a diagonal stitch from C back to A. Make the next vertical stitch from D to C and repeat the combination to the end of the line, ending with an upright stitch. Working from left to right on the second journey and using the same holes, make the vertical stitches over the top of the previous ones and slope the diagonals in the opposite direction.

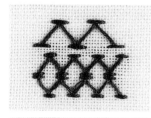

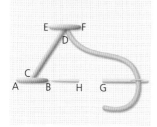

Chevron Stitch

A zigzag border stitch, this can also be worked in rows to create a diamond lattice (known as surface honeycomb in smocking). It is worked horizontally with alternating diagonal and horizontal stitches. Start with a back stitch from A to B. Bring the needle up midway along this stitch, at C. Make a slanting stitch up to the right, to D. Then make a back stitch from E to F. Come out again at D and make the next slanting stitch down to G. Repeat these four stitches to continue, starting below F, at H.

Back-Stitched Star

More of a cross than a star, this pretty stitch can be worked in rows, randomly, or as an isolated stitch. Carefully follow the threads on an evenweave material to create a symmetrical shape. Work the top right arm first, with three back stitches from A to B, C to A, and D to C. The other three arms are worked in the same way, the second arm starting from E to D and F to E.

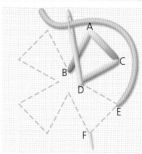

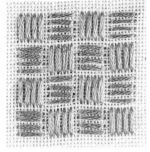 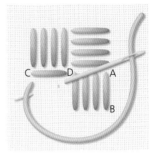

Basket Filling

This interesting stitch creates an interwoven texture, useful where a representational effect is needed. It is formed from straight stitches, arranged in alternating horizontal and vertical blocks. Work on evenweave fabric and keep the stitches regular. Begin the row with four parallel upright stitches, in the direction of A to B. The first stitches of the next block are worked in the direction of C to D. Repeat these two blocks to fill the required space.

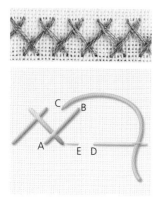

Herringbone Stitch

Work as a border or in rows as a diamond filling. Make a slanting stitch from A up to B. Bring the needle back up level with B, at C, and insert it at D. Come up again below B, at E. Continue by repeating these two crossed stitches.

Threaded Herringbone Stitch

Thread a tapestry needle with a contrasting thread to interlace a herringbone foundation. Come up at A and then slide the needle upward under the first stitch. Then slide it downward under the next stitch, at B. Continue to the end of the row.

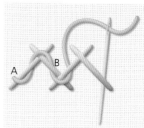

 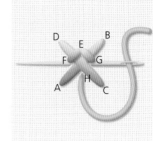

Square Boss Stitch

Work this raised stitch singly or in rows. The central square could be worked in a different color to vary the effect. Start with a cross stitch from A to B and C to D. Bring the needle out at E. Work a back stitch to F, then three more back stitches from G to E, H to G, and F to H to complete the square.

 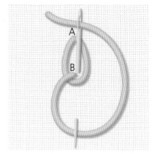

Chain Stitch (Tambour)

A flexible stitch, this is made up of a series of interlinked loops. It is useful for lettering and spirals as well as for outlines. Bring the needle up at A. Loop the thread from left to right and anchor it with a thumb. Insert the needle at A again and bring the point up at B, over the loop. Pull the thread through gently to make the first loop. Insert the needle at B again, inside the first loop, and repeat the sequence. Secure the final loop with a small straight stitch.

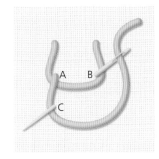

Open Chain Stitch (Ladder Stitch or Square Chain Stitch)

This can be varied by changing the width and height of the stitch, which explains the alternative names. Bring the needle up at A and take it down on the same level, at B, making a loop. Bring the point up at C, over the loop. Pull the thread through gently to make the first loop. Repeat the sequence to complete the line, and anchor the last loop with a short stitch at each corner.

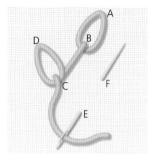

Feathered Chain Stitch

This stitch can be varied to change the angle and size of the stitches for a different look. Start with a slanting chain stitch (page 40) from A to B. Bring the needle up at B and make a long stitch to C. Come up at D to start the next chain stitch to C, slanting in the opposite direction. Make a long stitch from C to E and repeat the sequence from F to continue.

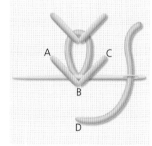

Wheat Ear Stitch

This naturalistic combination of straight and chain stitches is deceptively easy to work. Start with two diagonal stitches from A down to B and from C to B. Bring the needle up in a line below B, at D, and pass the needle behind the *V* of the previous two stitches. Insert the needle again at D to make a loop. Continue, alternating *V* shapes and chain stitches.

 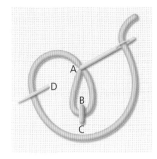

Detached Chain Stitch (Lazy Daisy Stitch)

Detached chain stitches can be worked singly or in a circle to create attractive flowers. Bring the needle up at the center point, A, and take it down again in the same hole. Bring it up at B and loop the thread from left to right, holding it down with a thumb tip and pulling the thread gently through and over the loop. Anchor the loop with a small straight stitch from B to C. Make the next stitch from A to D and continue clockwise to complete the flower.

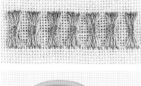

Sheaf Filling

A traditional filling, which can also be used singly, this stitch resembles an old-fashioned bundle of wheat. Start by working three parallel upright stitches from A to B, C to D, and E to F. Bring the needle out at G, behind the center of the second stitch, without piercing the thread. Slide the needle behind the stitches from right to left and take it back down at G. Draw the thread up carefully to pull the straight stitches together and finish off at the back.

Arrowhead Stitch (Arrow Stitch)

A simple V-shaped stitch, this can be used in rows as a border, singly as a filling, or to make geometric patterns. Make a diagonal stitch from A down to B. Bring the needle up at C and insert it again at B to complete the first "arrowhead." Start the next stitch directly below A, at D. Repeat the two diagonal stitches to the end for a vertical border, or start the next stitch next to C for a horizontal row.

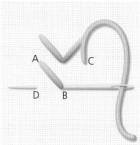

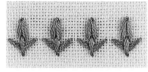

Tulip Stitch

A pretty floral stitch, this can be worked in rows or singly. Vary the height and width, or use two colors, for a different look. Start by making an arrowhead stitch from A to B and C to B. Bring the needle up at D, directly above B, and loop the thread from left to right. Take the needle back down at D and bring it up at E. Pull the thread gently to form the loop to make the flower head and take the needle down at F, directly below E, to complete the stalk.

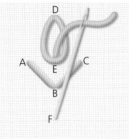

Blanket Stitch

A useful linear stitch that can also be used to finish an edge. Bring the needle up at A. Take it down again at B and come up directly below, at C, over the working thread. Repeat to continue, anchoring the final loop with a small straight stitch.

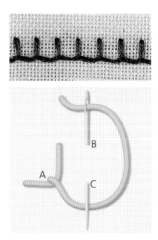

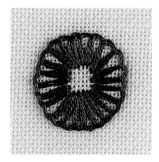 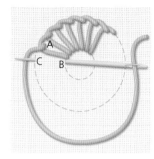

Buttonhole Wheel (Wheel Stitch)

Blanket stitch can be worked within a ring to make a spoked wheel, ideal for flowers, eyes, or as an isolated stitch. Keep the stitches closely spaced to prevent the outer threads from curling inward. Start by marking two circles on the fabric. Bring the needle up at A on the outside edge. Take the needle down at B on the inner circle and bring it up, over the working thread at C. Continue stitching counterclockwise, looping the final stitch under the first to complete the wheel.

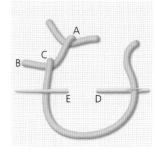

Open Cretan Stitch (Long-Armed Feather Stitch)

This spiky, looped stitch is worked from top to bottom and can be used in rows as a filling. Make a loose diagonal stitch from A to B. Bring the needle up over the thread and level with B, at C. Make a loose diagonal stitch from C to D. Bring the needle up over the thread and directly below A, at E. Repeat these two steps, stitching alternately to the right, then the left.

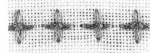

Four-Legged Knot

1. Resembling an upright cross stitch with a coral stitch at the center, this knot can be used on its own as an accent stitch or in groups as a scattered filling. Start with an upright straight stitch from A down to B. Bring the needle up at C and pass it under the first stitch, without pulling through the thread just yet. Loop the working thread over the stitch to the left and pass the needle over it as shown.

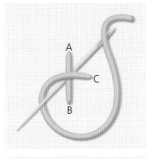

2. Gently pull the needle through and pull up the thread to create a knot. Take the needle back down at D to finish off.

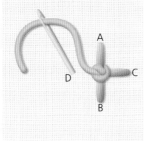

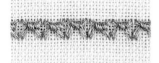

Sorbello

1. Work this Italian square knot in rows or as a filling. Work a straight stitch from A to B. Bring the needle up at C and pass it up under the first stitch. Holding the working thread to the left, slide the needle back down under the first stitch and over the working thread.

2. Gently pull the thread to form a knot, and finish by taking the needle back down at D.

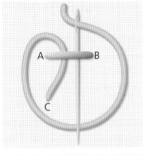

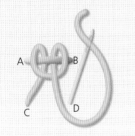

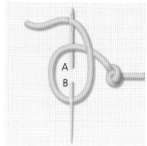

Coral Stitch (Snail Trail)

The alternative name of this linear stitch is wonderfully descriptive. The knots can be spaced closely or widely depending on the effect required. Insert the needle at A and loop the thread from left to right. Bring the needle up just below, at B, over the looped thread. Pull the thread through to form a small knot. Start the next stitch a short distance to the left.

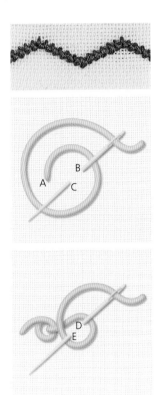

Scroll Stitch (Single Knotted Line Stitch)

1. This knotted linear stitch is worked from left to right. Bring the needle up at A and make a stitch up to the right, to B. Bring the point out at C so that the needle is angled. Wrap the thread clockwise under both ends of the needle.

2. Pull the thread through carefully, maintaining the round loop. Insert the needle at D and come out at E, ready to wrap the next loop. Continue in this way to the end of the line.

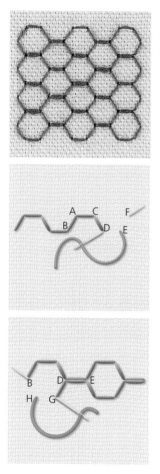

Honeycomb Filling

1. This open, hexagonal lattice is worked with two rows of stepped back stitch, sewn alternately forward and backward across the outline. Starting on the left, work four back stitches from A to B, C to A, D to C, E to D, etc., to the other side of the area to be filled.

2. Now work back across the area from right to left to make a mirror image with stitches from D to E, G to D, H to G, B to H, etc. Repeat these two rows until the required area is filled.

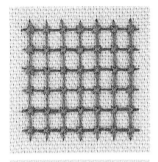

Jacobean Couching (Trellis Couching)

1. Lay the foundation grid by working two sets of parallel lines across the area to be filled. Start with long stitches from A to B, C to D, E to F, G to H, etc. Work the second set at right angles across the first from I to J, K to L, etc.

2. Work small cross stitches, from N to O and Q to P, and repeat across the horizontal rows to tie down the points where the long stitches intersect.

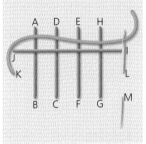

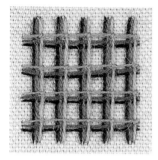 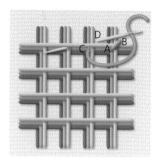

Battlement Couching

This is a development of Jacobean couching that has a raised, textured effect. Lay down three grids of stitches, each one positioned slightly above and to the right of the previous grid. Tie the top grid down, working small diagonal stitches from A to B, C to D, and so on in horizontal rows across the grid.

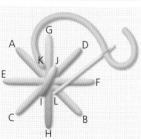

Star Filling

This round star is an effective isolated stitch, which can also be worked in rows or as a scattered filling. Work a diagonal cross stitch from A to B and then C to D, followed by a St. George cross (page 56) from E to F and G to H. Finish off with a small elongated cross over the center, worked from I to J and K to L. This tiny cross can be worked in a different color to give a flowerlike look to the stitch.

Ribbed Spider's Web (Raised Spoke Stitch)

This is an attractive accent stitch. Start with a large star filling stitch (page 54) but omit the small cross on top. Thread a blunt needle with a long length of the second color, and bring it up at the center of the star. Slide the needle to the left, under the first two stitches, then take it under the second and third stitches to make a back stitch. Continue until only the tips of the star can be seen beyond the raised ribs and finish the thread off at the back.

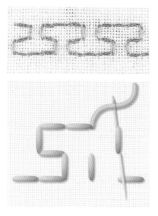

Holbein Stitch (Chiara Stitch)

Made up of two rows of running stitches worked into the same holes, this stitch, taken from counted thread work, looks the same on both the right and the wrong side of the fabric. It is used especially for lines and fillings. Intricate patterns, in one or two colors, can be charted on graph paper. For the first journey, work every other stitch, like a running stitch (page 25), along the design. On the return, fill in the spaces between them, angling the needle slightly to create a smooth line.

St. George Cross Stitch

This is simply a basic cross stitch set "en pointe," which can be used as a random filling, in rows to form a geometric pattern, or as an isolated accent stitch. Start with a horizontal stitch from A across to B. Bring the needle up at C and insert it directly below at D to finish the cross. Always sew the horizontal before the upright stitch, especially when working in rows.

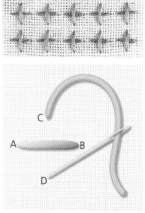

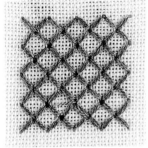
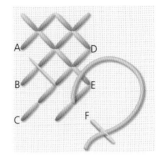

Back Stitch Trellis

This geometric filling produces an open diamond grid, which can be light or dense depending on the thickness of the thread and the length of the stitches. Work a series of parallel diagonal rows of back stitch (page 26) from right to left, starting with row A and working down to row E. Then work the back stitches to complete the trellis, also in parallel diagonal rows, but at right angles to the first ones, starting with row D and working down to row F.

 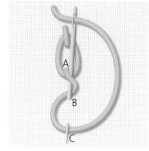

Cable Chain Stitch

This interlinked chain takes a little practice, but can easily be mastered. Bring the needle up at A. Hold the thread down with a thumb to keep it taut. Pass the point of the needle under the thread from right to left, and then back over the thread to the right. Keeping the working thread under the needle, insert the needle at B and bring it up at C, again over the thread. Pull the loop up gently to form an interconnecting straight stitch and loop.

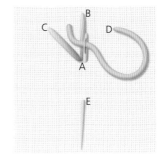

Fern Stitch

This pretty stitch can be worked geometrically, with all the stitches the same length, or freely to create more naturalistic foliage. It consists of three straight stitches that all radiate from the same point. Bring the needle up at A and make a straight stitch up to B. Then come up at C and work a diagonal stitch down to A. Complete with a stitch from D to A. Start the next group of stitches at E, directly below A.

Detached Wheat Ear Stitch (Tete-de-boeuf Stitch or Oxhead Stitch)

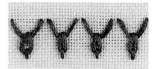

A combination of fly and detached chain stitches, this pretty filling is used in crewel work and as an isolated stitch. Make a loose stitch from A to B. Bring the needle up over the thread halfway between A and B, at C. Take the needle back down at C, holding a loop of thread with the thumb, and bring the point out directly below, at D and over the loop. Pull the thread through and draw up the loop to make a chain. Secure it with a small straight stitch.

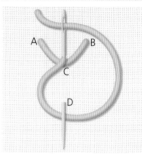

 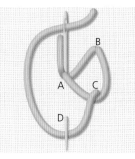

Chained Feather Stitch

This heavier variation of feather stitch has an interlinked appearance. Bring the needle up at A and make a loose diagonal stitch up to B. Bring the point out over the thread at C, directly below B, and gently pull the thread through. Take the needle down again at A and come up at D over the looped thread. Insert the needle again at C to start the next stitch, then repeat this alternating pattern to the end. Finish with a small stitch to secure the loop.

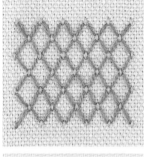

Cloud Filling (Mexican Filling)

1. This interlaced filling is woven over a foundation of small, upright stitches. Work the first row of regularly spaced foundation stitches from A to B, C to D, etc across the area to be filled. Work the second row in the same way, but with each stitch midway between the stitches above. With a second color, come up at E. Slide the needle under stitch AB, under the next stitch on the row below, under stitch CD, and so on to the end of the row.

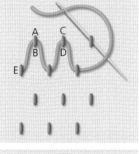

2. Start the next row at F and continue lacing in the same way, but in the opposite direction, to complete the row. Continue in the same way to lace through all the foundation stitches.

Pearl Stitch

1. This gives a flexible knotted outline, resembling a string of beads. Make a short diagonal stitch from A up to B. Bring the needle up below B and level with A, at C. Slide the needle from right to left under the stitch and the loop, then gently pull the thread to form a small knot.

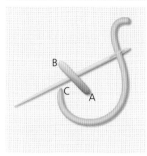

2. Take the needle down just to the left of B at D to create the next diagonal stitch from C. Come up at E ready for the next knot.

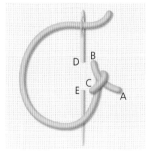

Knotted Chain Stitch (Link Stitch)

1. A heavily textured stitch that works best with thick threads, this is a cross between pearl and chain stitches. Make a small angled stitch from A down to B and bring the needle up below A, at C. Slip the needle downward under the angled stitch, then under the loop and over the working thread.

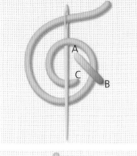

2. Pull the thread through to form a loose knot to the left of the straight stitch and continue working to the left.

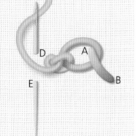